CANADA

BOOK OF

DECREES & PROPHECIES

Graphic design by Faytene Grasseschi.

Published by V-Kol Media Ministries.
Printed by Lightning Source.
ISBN: 978-0-9891017-1-4

With Written Contributions By

(Listed alphabetically by first name.)

Alain Caron
Brendan Witton
Brent Sloss
Bill Prankard
Derek Schneider
Doug Schneider
Faytene Grasseschi
Femi & Remi Ogunrinde
Giulio Lorefice Gabeli
Patricia Bootsma
Patricia King
Peg Byars
Peggy Kennedy
Rob & Fran Parker
Wanda Fost

Dedicated to:

The great heroes of the faith in Canada who
have prayerfully and faithfully stood for the Gospel.

Special Thanks:

To God for His abundant mercy and generosity
shown towards the nation of Canada.

To each of the contributors.

To KC McLean, Ashley Beaudin and Veronique Golloher
for your wonderful editing assistance.

To all those who have faithfully decreed
God's Word over Canada throughout the years.

Table of Contents

PREFACE

Welcome to Canada Book of Decrees and Prophecies. We are honoured that you have joined with us to pray for the nation of Canada through these pages. We absolutely believe in the power of unified prayer. In addition, like you, we love God and love Canada! That is why this book exists. We pray that it will be a powerful tool, for the Body of Christ in Canada and beyond, to come into tangible agreement for God's blessing and for His fullness to come to this nation. We believe that as we come together in united prayer - whether by meeting at physical gatherings or in more unconventional ways, like through the pages of this book - we will see great results. God answers united prayer. Because of this we are full of faith.

In Matthew 18:19, Jesus shared this with His disciples:

> ...I tell you that if two of you on earth agree
> about anything you ask for, it will be done
> for you by my Father in heaven.

In this text the word *agree* is the greek word *sumphoneo*. It means to harmonize or come into agreement with one another. Jesus was telling His faithful disciples that as they came into harmony with one another regarding issues in the earth, and made requests to God in that spirit of harmony, their prayers would be answered by the Father in Heaven.

In the same way, we believe that as those who love and follow Jesus (e.g. His disciples in Canada) come into agreement with one another for His will to be done, something powerful will break forth. That something is answered prayer. In addition to the powerful principle of agreement, we also believe in the powerful principal of spoken decree.

Proverbs 18:21 teaches us that there is death and life in the power of the tongue and that we will eat the fruit of what we speak. James chapter three reiterates this when it says that a person's tongue is like the rudder of a boat or a small spark that sets an entire forest on fire. It is small but has great power. What we speak and declare has great effect!

Job 22:22-28 says it this way:

> Receive, I pray thee, the law from his
> mouth, and lay up his words in thine heart...
> For then shalt thou have thy delight in the
> Almighty, and shalt lift up thy face unto
> God. Thou shalt make thy prayer unto him,
> and he shall hear thee, and thou shalt pay thy
> vows. Thou shalt also decree a thing, and it
> shall be established unto thee: and the light
> shall shine upon thy ways. (NKJV)

These scriptures show us that as we are in alignment with
God and we speak forth His heart (decree it) then it will be
established.

The word *established* in this text is the Hebrew word
quwm, which means to be fixed, set in place, ratified, built,
brought onto the scene and to be made binding. This is
extremely powerful. For this reason we have formatted the
prayers of this book not simply as petitions to God, but as
decrees that we can harmonize on (Mt. 18:19), speak forth
(Prov. 18:21) and see established!

To this end, the following sections of this book contain powerful decrees written by several respected leaders from across Canada. Each section covers a different topic such as the harvest, unity in the Church, government, the generations and the like. As the various contributors have submitted their hearts to God in the writing of these decrees, we believe that they are in alignment with His will and therefore will be established as we pray them in agreement.

A Note About The Book's Format: In the editing and formatting of this book we have worked hard to preserve the unique writing of each contributor. For this reason you will notice a variety of styles from section to section. In addition, due to the fact that each decree is meant to be read in a continuous flow of prayer, we have intentionally left paragraph breaks out.

We invite you to engage in decreeing each section in a spirit of faith. As you do, you can be confident that you are joining in agreement with many others in powerful harmony and that these fervent and faith filled prayers will avail much (James 5:16).

Finally, in the last section of this book you will find transcripts of some of the recognized prophetic words that have been spoken over Canada. Because some of the decrees refer to these prophecies, we wanted to be sure to include them here for your reference. Please feel free to not only read them, but join with us in praying into them in a Spirit of faith. We do this knowing that, if we believe these words and call them forth, we shall prosper and they will come to pass (2 Chronicles 20:20).

We believe that God has given the pen of history into the hands of His praying Church. Thank you so much for joining with us to write history through faith filled prayer and decrees over Canada. Let's lay hold of His promises and fullness for this amazing nation!

Blessings in Christ,

Faytene Grasseschi

Director of TheCRY Movement,
MY Canada & V-Kol Media Ministries

The Power of The Cross

Faytene Grasseschi

Lord God, thank You for the Cross of Jesus Christ and its power. We declare in agreement with Your Word that the Cross holds the power of salvation for all men and all creation (Romans 1:16). By faith right now we loose the revelation of the power of the Cross of Jesus Christ over the nation of Canada. From the north tips, to the southern border, to the eastern coast, to the western coast we declare that the Cross of Jesus Christ is prevailing in demonstrative power. We decree that even this day the eyes of men and women from sea to sea in Canada are being opened to see the power of the Cross and that they are coming to the saving knowledge of Jesus Christ. Soften hearts all across this nation today, we pray. We declare that the power of the Cross is stronger than sickness, dysfunction and every form of darkness in Canada. We decree that Your Cross is prevailing over every region and way that the enemy is attempting to steal, kill or destroy in this nation (John 10:10). We decree that Your people are laying hold afresh of the power of the Cross and effectively applying it in all situations for Your name's sake and glory. Lord, we thank You that You love Canada. We acknowledge that You declared to Your Son, Jesus Christ, "Ask of me and I will give You the nations as Your inheritance" (Psalm 2:8). We believe that He is asking for Canada. We thank You that when He died on the Cross, that He had Canada in mind and that He came to destroy all the work of the devil in this nation (1 John 3:8). We thank You for the destiny on the nation of Canada. We believe that You put it in the hearts of our Founding Fathers and that it was echoed through them as they chose to call Canada the Dominion of Canada, after Psalm 72:8, declaring that He would have dominion from sea to sea. We echo this decree today over our nation. We lift up Your Cross and declare that Your goodness, truth and ways will prevail across the land. We loose the power of the Cross and thank You that the glory of Your mercy and truth will triumph in power from sea to sea in Canada. Let Your Kingdom come in Canada as it is in Heaven. We decree and loose all these things in the mighty name of Jesus. Amen.

Revival of the Word of God

Brent Sloss

In the mighty and powerful name of Jesus, we decree that the Body of Christ is richly receiving the Word of Christ. Your Word is like fire shut up in our bones! Father, we ask You to make Your ministers flames of fire (Hebrews 1:7) and set us ablaze by the fire of God. Holy Spirit, we ask that You would grant the Body of Christ in Canada ears to hear, eyes to see, and a heart to perceive and understand what You are saying to the Church (Revelation 2:29). We thank You that You are stirring up a fresh hunger for the Word of God and that they are releasing a fresh word from God. Father, we thank You for a revival of the Word of God in Canada. We decree that where truth lies fallen in the streets (Isaiah 59:14), there is a people who are picking it up and running swiftly with it. Stir up a zeal! Stir up zeal! Stir up a zeal! Let the zeal of a few stir up the majority. We decree that they are boldly speaking a due word in due season (Isaiah 50:4). Lord, we ask You to thrust out labourers into Canada to declare Your Word boldly (Luke 10:2). Send out Your light, send out Your truth and let them lead us Lord (Psalm 43:3)! We declare that the Word of God is living and powerful (Hebrews 4:12). Father, thank You that Canada shall be filled with the knowledge of the Glory of God (Habakkuk 2:14). We decree that the knowledge of Jesus is being diffused through every believer in every place. Run swiftly, children of God, with a grace to run the race! Do your part until every heart believes He is the Way! Holy Spirit, we "...pray that the Master's Word will simply take off and race through the country to a groundswell of response, just as it has among us..." (2 Thes. 3:1, MSG). Father, grant to Your people that with all boldness they may speak Your Word (Acts 4:29). We say, like Mary, "Be it unto us, according to your Word," (Luke 1:38) in Canada, to Canada, and for Canada. We say that the Word of God is spreading and the number of disciples is multiplying in Jesus' name. Canada arise! Canada shall be saved!

Repentance & Awakening

Femi and Remi Ogunrinde

Father, we come humbly before You to corporately and individually repent for apathy, complacency and indifference. We pray according to 2 Chronicles 7:14, which says, "if My people, who are called by My name, will humble themselves and pray and seek My face and turn from their wicked ways, then will I hear from Heaven and will forgive their sin and will heal their land." We acknowledge that we have often deviated from the path of righteousness. Instead, we have often walked in apathy and complacency, and this has ruled our churches at times. We also acknowledge the cold heart and indifference to personal sins and the sins of our nation that we have had a times. We repent and ask for Your forgiveness and for cleansing. Therefore having obtained mercy (2 Corinthians 4:1), we put You to remembrance of Your promise to heal our land. We declare and decree a great move of God across our nation and a great awakening for Your Church. Just as Your Church was birthed apostolically, we declare that this 'Last Days' Church in Canada will overturn the wicked powers of darkness and light will shine once again through us. Father, we thank You for the great moves of God from Canada that have impacted the earth, for the promises to the Puritan reformers, and the promises through prophecies of Charles Price, David Yonggi-Cho and many other prophetic voices.[1] In the matchless name of our Lord, we decree an end to drought and famine and call forth abundant rain upon every soul. Your Word declares that in the Last Days You will pour out of Your Spirit upon all flesh (Joel 2:28-32). We call this forth for Canada. Father, we pray that Your Kingdom would come and Your will would be done on earth in Canada, just as it is in Heaven (Matthew 6:10). We ask for the rain in the time of the latter rain (Hosea 6:3). We call forth the rain Lord! Open the floodgates of Heaven (Malachi 3:10). We declare that the Church is infused with power. We are alive and well! Your Church in Canada is taking her commission seriously. We declare that the Church You purchased freely with Your blood is glorious, triumphant and manifesting Christ while reforming and transforming society.

The Harvest

Brendan Witton

Father, we thank You for Your heart for the multitudes of people in our nation. We thank You that You are not slow regarding Your promise but that You are patient towards us, not wishing for any to perish but all to come to repentance (2 Peter 3:9). We agree with Your Word and lift up our eyes and look on the fields, that they are white for harvest (John 4:35). Just as You were, Jesus, we see the multitudes and are moved with compassion for them, because they are like sheep without a shepherd (Mathew 9:36). We declare that Your people in Canada are compelled to action because of Your compassion that burns in their hearts. We agree with Your Word that the harvest is plentiful (Matthew 9:37) and ask that You would thrust forth the labourers into Your harvest (Matthew 9:38)! We declare in Jesus' name that there is an abundance of harvest workers in our nation. We declare that Canadian harvest workers are being released to the nations to bring life and healing! Father, send forth the labourers! Send forth the labourers! We declare that we will not grow weary in sowing seed and doing good, for

Your Word promises that You will not be mocked; for whatever a man sows he will also reap (Galatians 6:7, 9). We thank You for the seeds of the Gospel that have been sown in our nation. We thank You for the seeds of intercession that have been sown in our nation. We thank You and declare that those seeds will come forth in harvest in Jesus' name! Father, we declare and thank You for an unprecedented, supernatural, net-breaking, boat-sinking harvest that will sweep through our nation and then to the nations of the world in Jesus' name!

The Father's Heart

Patricia Bootsma

"How great is the love the Father has lavished on us, that
we should be called children of God! And
that is what we are!" (1 John 3:1)

We pray and decree over Canada the release of revelation
of the Father's love for every individual and over every
geographical area of our nation. We embrace the spirit of
sonship, forsaking every orphan tendency. We receive
healing as a nation for insecurity, independence and
pharisaical mindsets. We enter into the rest of knowing we
are children of a loving Father. We acknowledge our need
for our Father and depend on His work in our lives and
nation. We decree that we live by the law of love. We
declare that the saints in Canada comprehend the width and
length and depth and height of the love of Christ so we may
be filled with all the fullness of God entering into the
"...exceedingly abundantly above all we ask or think
according to the power that works in us," (Ephesians
3:18-20). We loose the Father's love to touch every

fatherless child, every politician, every mother and father, factory worker and tradesman. We declare that the love of the Father is becoming a reality of the heart for every person in Canada – not just a mental concept. We decree that the Father's love touches every city, every province and territory and that love spills out into the streets and prisons, courtrooms and political offices. As Canadians, we enter into faith, we enter into hope, but we especially enter into love – the greatest of these (1 Corinthians 13:13).

Signs & Wonders

Brent Sloss

In the mighty name of Jesus, we thank You Father that You are building a people of power. You are building a people of praise! We decree that the people of God are walking in signs and wonders. We are confident about You! Holy Spirit, we ask that we may know You and the power of the resurrection (Philippians 3:10). We declare that those who know You are strong and walk in the power of Your might (Daniel 11:32). Jesus, we thank You that we are Your people, called by Your name (Isaiah 43:7). Thank You for working with us, confirming Your Word with signs and wonders following (Mark 16:20). We believe that we are Your partners and You are showing Yourself strong with signs and wonders, with miracles, and gifts of the Spirit. We decree we are filled with faith and full of power. We declare that the people of God are walking in Your powerful authority to 'be' and explosive authority to 'do'. Thank You for pouring out Your Spirit and we declare Your Word that signs will follow those who believe (Mark 16:17). We declare that old men are dreaming dreams, young men are seeing visions (Acts 2:17), the lame are walking, the blind seeing, and the dead are being raised (Matthew 11:5). We call for the Body of Christ to arise to fulfill the call of God on her life! Holy Spirit, we ask that Your communion would be with every believer. We ask for a continual encounter with Holy Spirit. We pray for a release of revelation that Jesus has sent Holy Spirit to be our Helper and demonstrate the supernatural (John 15:26). Lord, we believe! We receive Your gifts. We are awakened by Your love and strengthened by Your might! Glory!

Righteousness

Derek Schneider

Father, we come to You now in the name of Jesus, petitioning You for the Spirit of Righteousness to visit this nation! We, the Church, come to You first in a posture of repentance for arrogance, passivity, and religiosity. We repent of our sins. We repent for turning from a pursuit of holiness and a hunger for righteousness, to accepting a spirit of complacency and compromise. Forgive us God, for becoming so comfortable with stale Christianity and unrighteousness. We, the Church in this nation, have left our post and allowed unrighteousness in our churches, and ultimately in society. We repent for this today. Father, pour out Your Spirit of reformation upon the Church in this nation again! Call us back to holiness. Restore us as gatekeepers of this land, and may every sphere of society be influenced by Your Church as we hunger and thirst for righteousness (Matthew 5:6). We say to You today, that we will not stop praying, we will not stop seeking You, and we will not stop labouring, until righteousness is established in our land and this nation is exalted (Proverbs 14:34)! We call upon You, Holy Spirit, to fuel this reformation of the Church until Canada is shaken by the presence of our God. We are calling for a reformation that displays Your power to this nation. We cry out to You Lord. We ask that You would reform us until we, Your Church, emerge in true apostolic grace and authority. Canada belongs to You Lord. Establish us in righteousness (Proverbs 14:34). We ask that You would clothe us with a garment of holiness. May the Canadian Church lead in righteousness. May Your Kingdom have dominion from sea to sea (Psalm 72:8)! Amen.

Justice

Faytene Grasseschi

Father, thank You that righteousness and justice are the foundation of Your throne (Psalm 89:14). We understand that Your throne is where you sit and dwell. We desire that Canada would be Your dwelling place, and so, because of this, we fervently lay hold of righteousness and justice for our nation right now as we pray. We thank You that where Your justice is active, wrongs are made right. This means that the broken are mended, the poor are fed and the vulnerable are protected. We rejoice in Your justice (Psalm 98:9) and we loose the prevailing power of Your justice to roll back every injustice that exists in Canada! We speak specifically to the issues of human trafficking, abortion, elder abuse, domestic abuse extortion, corruption, terrorism, racism and all forms of exploitation - we loose justice in the name of Jesus. We ask that those who perpetuate injustices would be swiftly brought to salvation, filled with Holy Spirit and would change their ways. We loose words of knowledge and revelation to all of our law officials, to enable them to discover, and restrain, those who are perpetuating injustices. We also decree that the eyes of civilians are being opened to see where injustices are happening and they are promptly acting to report them. Raise up a generation of rescuers and establishers of biblical justice all across our land. Father, where our laws do not reflect Your heart for justice, we now loose revelation and courage into the hearts of our legislators to change them. We decree this at the municipal, provincial, federal and all judicial levels in the name of Jesus. We decree that our laws will reflect Heaven's heart. We decree this specifically for the issue of abortion right now in Jesus' name. Father, we acknowledge that the status quo of legal abortion from conception to full gestation (9 mos.) grieves Your heart, and for this we repent before You now. We ask that You would arise on behalf of Canada's unborn. We declare in faith that the tide is swiftly turning, and we loose the spirit of justice into Canada on this issue in particular. Raise up justice reformers with strategy and favour in every sphere of society! Turn the scales towards biblical justice in our nation. We declare that Canada is swiftly becoming an example of Your heart for justice to the world. With all the faith we have, we now loose the spirit of justice into our entire nation.

Favour

Patricia King

We thank You that in Christ Jesus Canada is favoured by Heavenly Father. We thank You that as Canada turns to You, the favour You have given Your Son has been given to Canada as well. This is undeserved, unmerited favour that is granted to Canada in Christ. We thank You that Your favour is a free gift to Canada, for which we are very thankful. We ask that You would draw Canadians to receive this free gift today (John 6:44). As Jesus kept increasing in wisdom and stature, and in favour with God and men (Luke 2:52), we declare that Canada does also, because she abides in Jesus and He abides in her (John 15:7). We declare that Canada embraces the favour of God, for it is better than silver and gold (Proverbs 22:1). We ask You for Your enduring favour. We thank You that Your favour endures for a lifetime (Psalm 30:5) and causes her mountains of influence and blessing to stand strong. We decree that the Lord's favour surrounds Canada like a shield against Canada's enemies (Psalm 5:12). We call forth Your favour which releases Your vindication and delights in Canada's prosperity. We thank You that Your blessing upon Canada attracts the rich among the people who seek the favour of Canada. We ask that by the favour and wisdom of the Lord, all of Canada's works and decisions would be confirmed and established (Psalm 90:17). We declare that everything Canada puts her hands to for righteousness sake (Psalm 90:17), is favoured; that her steps are bathed in butter and the rock pours out oil for Canada (Job 29:6). As Canada seeks the Lord's favour, He is gracious unto her according to His Word. We declare that Canada's citizens are highly favoured in their homes and favoured in the workplace. They are favoured everywhere they go and in all that they do. We declare that Canada's leaders and citizens love wisdom and seek diligently for wisdom and understanding (Proverbs 4:5). Therefore Canada has been granted favour by the Lord and is greatly favoured by others. In the light of the King's face is life, and His favour is like a cloud with the spring rain over Canada (Proverbs 16:15). His favour is like heavenly dew that falls upon all of Canada. We thank You that Canada is favoured in God's presence and the Lord goes before Canada's leaders and citizens revealing His goodness and glory to Canada (Exodus 33:19). His favour opens doors of opportunity for Canada that no man can shut (Isaiah 45:1). By His favour through Christ, Canada has been granted the keys of the Kingdom and whatever we bind on earth is bound in Heaven. Whatever we loose on earth has been loosed in Heaven (Matthew 18:18). We thank You that through Christ His righteous scepter of favour is extended towards Canada. Whatever Canada asks in the name of Christ, He grants unto Canada, when we make our requests and petitions according to His will (John 15:7). Lord, we thank You that You daily grant Canada great favour because of the covenant blood of Christ and the promises in His Word. Blessed be the Lord who gives favour!

Blessing

Patricia King

We decree that Canada has been created for blessing and as a blessing. The maple leaf on the Canadian flag reflects the calling Canada has to bring healing to the nations (Revelation 22:2). As a result, we declare that Canada is fruitful in every good thing, multiplies and increases in blessings (Colossians 1:10). Because God has blessed Canada, we declare that no curse can touch her (Isaiah 54:17). In the name of Jesus Christ and by the power of His blood, we decree His covenant of blessing around Canada's borders and all that pertains to this nation. We declare that nothing but blessing is permitted to come into Canada and her sphere of influence. If the enemy attempts to attack Canada, he will be caught in the act and pay sevenfold what he stole -- then his house shall be plundered, for Canada only accepts blessings (Proverbs 6:31). We thank You Lord that the enemy's attempts to destroy only create testimonies of God's increased blessings for Canada (Romans 8:28). Like Abraham,

Canada is blessed and is called to be a blessing (Genesis 22:18). Through the Church in Canada, nations are blessed. As Canada walks faithfully before the Lord, we decree that blessings come upon Canada and overtake her and that blessings are attracted to Canada (Deuteronomy 28:2). We loose blessings over Canada as she is coming in and going out (Deuteronomy 28:6). We declare blessings over all of Canada's cities, provinces and all of Canada's fields. We call forth the open heavens over Canada, the rain of God's abundant goodness to fall upon Canada and all that pertains to her. We thank You God that no good thing have You withheld from Canada (Psalm 84:11). We call forth Your blessing on everything Canada puts her hand to for Your name's sake. We loose a blessing over all of Canada's households, food, clothing, vehicles, business and matters of business. We decree blessing over the children, family, and all who labour within Canada and for Canada. We decree a blessing over Canada's finances and economy (Deuteronomy 28:4). We thank You that Jesus established an eternal, unbreakable covenant of blessing when He died on the Cross and rose again. We declare that the eyes of Canadians are being opened on mass to this saving grace and Canadians are walking in the ways of the Lord. We declare Canada is blessed with the Kingdom of Heaven and its bounty because she recognizes the need of God in all things and at all times. We decree Canada is blessed with comfort when she mourns and a satisfied heart because she hungers and thirsts for righteousness (Matthew 5:6). We declare that Canada is blessed with mercy because she shows mercy to others and that Canada is blessed with insights and visitations from God because she is pure in spirit (Matthew 5:8). We declare that Canada is called a 'Nation of God' because Canada is a peacemaker (Matthew 5:9). When Canada is persecuted for the sake of righteousness or when people insult her and speak lies about Canada, she is blessed with heavenly and eternal reward (Matthew 5:11). Canada is blessed because she hears the Lord's Word and acts on it. Canada is a doer of the Word and not a hearer only (James 1:22). We decree that Canada loves wisdom and righteousness therefore she is highly blessed (Proverbs 4:6). The blessing of the Lord will make Canada rich and the Lord will adds no sorrow to it (Proverbs 10:22). We declare that Canada trusts in the Lord and because of this she is highly blessed. Canada is blessed with every spiritual blessing in the heavenly places in Christ

(Ephesians 1:3). Grace and peace are multiplied unto Canada in the knowledge of Christ (2 Peter 1:2). We declare that Canada has been granted everything that pertains to life and to godliness (2 Peter 1:3). Canada has been given all the magnificent promises in the Word of God. Canada sows blessings bountifully and therefore she reaps blessings bountifully. We decree that Canada always looks for ways she can bless others. The Lord blesses Canada, indeed, and enlarges her realms of influence. His hand of grace and blessing is with Canada, and He keeps Canada from harm (Psalm 121:7). We declare that Canada is truly blessed in all things, for God in Heaven has chosen gladly to give unto Canada the Kingdom (Luke 12:32). Thank You Lord that You bless Canada continuously and cause Your face to shine upon her. You are gracious unto Canada and grant her peace (Numbers 6:24-26).

Church Leadership

Brendan Witton

Father, we thank You for Your leaders in Your Church here in Canada. We thank You for the apostles, prophets, evangelists, pastors and teachers in Your people (Ephesians 4:11). We thank You for those who lead with Your heart in the seven mountains of church, family, government, business, education, media, arts and entertainment. We bless them today in Jesus' name! We thank You that You are filling them with the spirit of wisdom and revelation in the knowledge of You (Ephesians 1:17). We declare that the eyes of their hearts are enlightened so they may know what is the hope of their calling, what are the riches of the glory of Your inheritance in the saints, and what is the surpassing greatness of Your power towards them as they believe (Ephesians 1:17-19). We declare that You are granting them, according to the riches of Your glory, to be strengthened with power through Your Spirit in their inner man. Thank You that Christ is dwelling in their hearts through faith, and that they will be rooted and grounded in Your love. We declare that they will be able to comprehend with all the saints what is the breadth and length and height and depth, and know the love of Christ which surpasses knowledge, that they may be filled up to all the fullness of You (Ephesians 3:16-19)! We declare blessing over their marriages! We declare blessing over their children! We declare that no weapon formed against them shall prosper and every tongue that rises against them in judgment will be shown to be in the wrong (Isaiah 54:17)! We thank You that they are strong in You and in the power of Your might and stand firm against all the schemes of the enemy (Ephesians 6:10-11). We declare that they are strong and courageous and that Your Word will not depart from their mouths but they will meditate on it day and night (Joshua 1:7-8). We declare that the fire of their first love for You continues to burn strongly in their hearts (Revelation 2:4) and that like David they will serve Your purpose in their generation in Jesus' name (Acts 13:36)!

Spiritual Fathers

Giulio Lorefice Gabeli

Father we thank You that You are our Abba, our Daddy (Romans 8:15)! You have always been there for us, You have never left us nor forsaken us (Deuteronomy 31:6); You have always been faithful and consistent, constant in your love as a Father (Hebrews 13:8)! Lord we pray that You will awaken true spiritual fathers; who will arise in our nation with a genuine calling to father and mentor young men in our nation. God, we pray that they will confront the orphan spirit that is plaguing the Church and restore the transparency and credibility for the generations to walk together! Lord, we pray that these leaders will catch the vision of passing on the baton to next generation without fear of losing their prominence or position. Lord, we pray that they will pour into the younger leaders without any personal agendas or selfish motives. May they embrace the true heart of a servant, serving the Kingdom of God by preparing young emerging leaders with genuine love and commitment.

Father we thank You that, "...you are restoring the hearts of the fathers back to the children and the hearts of the children back to the fathers..." according to Malachi 4:6. Thank You Lord that these spiritual fathers will model the heart of our Heavenly Father redeeming what has been lost in the generational gaps through out the Church and our nation! We declare that these spiritual fathers, "...will rebuild the ancient ruins and will raise up the age-old foundations; [they] will be called Repairer of Broken Walls, Restorer of Streets with Dwellings." (Isaiah 58:12) We declare that these spiritual fathers will be a covering of safety and protection willingly laying down their lives for the next generation (John 15:13)! We declare that they will be passionate lovers of God displaying an intimacy with God that will inspire younger leaders to love the Lord of the ministry over the work of the ministry!

Spiritual Mothers

Wanda Fost

In the precious name of our Lord Jesus Christ we pray and decree:

We call the true identity of the spiritual mothers of the nation to come forth in the fullness of esteem and favour of God. We declare that they will walk in zeal as they are provoked by the immeasurable love of God (2 Corinthians 5:14). They will be defiant against the enemy and assertive in battle. We declare, the spiritual mothers in Canada are alive and well, a supernatural force that is unstoppable. With open eyes they see the inheritance of the next generation and see from Heaven's perspective. Awakened, they stand declaring in the same spirit that Deborah did saying, "When I Deborah saw my city was in ruin, I arose as a mother in the land!" They stand firm believing for the true identity of Jesus to fill this nation. They draw wisdom from God as that of the sons of Issachar who accurately discerned the times (1 Chronicles 12:32). We decree that they pray from Heaven's perspective, a place of peace and rest, knowing God stands with them. They fearlessly fight for the family, refusing to be defeated. They stand in the gap interceding, believing all mountains and barriers will crumble and the true family of God will come forth. With no cracks in their armor, they walk with immovable faith and courage that is contagious. We thank You that they fight for the children, call home the prodigals and break the orphan spirit. We declare these spiritual mothers to be joy givers, faith builders and life releasers. They are those who declare, "All [our] sons will be taught by the LORD, and great will be [our] children's peace." (Isaiah 54:13). We pray that this force of women will live in a dimension that is vastly different then that of the world - rising with an apostolic anointing establishing and building the Kingdom of God in every corner of this nation. We declare they are birthing the fullness of His glory, bringing healing and bringing restoration. They are midwifing the fullness of all that God has planned and purposed. We declare these spiritual mothers will set a Godly example with strong Christian character. With unshakable and immovable faith these warriors will help teach and lead the Body into its true identity. We declare this force will never let go and that for them quitting is not an option. Mothers of Canada arise! We pray this in the mighty Name of our Lord and Saviour Jesus Christ. Amen.

Families

Femi & Remi Ogunrinde

Lord, we acknowledge that the family is the unit through which You have perpetuated Your dominion mandate (Genesis 1:28). We thank You that it is through You that the whole family in Heaven and Earth is named (Ephesians 3:15). In the mighty name of Jesus, we declare and decree that our families are blessed with every spiritual blessing in the heavenly places in Christ Jesus (Ephesians 1:3). We decree and declare the authority of God's Word that our families are mighty in the land and that this generation of the upright will be blessed (Psalm 112:2). We proclaim and declare that through skillful and godly wisdom our families are built; and by understanding it is established on sound and good foundation (Proverbs 24:3). We declare and stand for Your view of marriage and of family and contend for this righteous foundation. Therefore we decree that the house of the uncompromisingly righteous shall stand (Proverbs 12:7). We ask for Your forgiveness as a nation where we have tried to re-define what family is all about.

We come against every assignment that has tried to threaten this foundation of our society. We decree that the Lord has broken every yoke off the necks of every family in Canada and burst every band of the wicked, that our families may serve the Lord; therefore, we loose every yoke and every band off all our families in Jesus' name (Matthew 18:18). We declare and decree that as for us and our household we would serve and worship the Lord (Joshua 24:15). We acknowledge You as Lord over our families. We thank You that You delight in the prosperity of Your people. We declare that Canadian families flourish in this prosperity and welfare (Psalm 35:27).

Next Generation

Derek Schneider

Father in the Name of Jesus we come to You today, thanking You for a generation sold out for You in Canada! We take a moment first to thank You for those who have gone before, us and the sacrifice they made to prepare the way for the next generation. We honour them and say thank You Lord for such an inheritance! Now, Spirit of the Lord, we come into agreement right now for the next generation. We pray that righteousness and integrity would be the foundation of everything they do. We pray that they would be those who walk in the spirit of Josiah, and bring true reform in their day. On their watch may the ending of abortion become a reality in Canada! May they walk in a spirit of honour, the spirit of Elisha, and may they destroy the power of Jezebel in this nation. May true authority be the platform on which they establish Your Kingdom and may the harvest be given into their hands. Holy Spirit, we call for the reformers, and history makers to be raised up - those without compromise and the kind of which it was said that "the world was not worthy of [them]..." (Hebrews

11:38). We call them forward in the spirit to take their place as deliverers in this land. Let young kings and judges arise. We declare over the next generation, that through them a nation will not only be transformed, but that righteousness will be systemic in our land. We declare that they will possess the land (Leviticus 20:24)! We declare that the sins of the fathers will not become their sins, and that signs and wonders will follow them in an unprecedented way (Mark 16:17). Let every sector of society be shaken by the sound of young giants walking through this land. We decree that they will be those who walk in a love relationship with their God, but will make war against compromise, principalities and every form of wickedness. Father, let them look like Your Son, and may they answer the groaning of a world waiting for the manifestation of the "sons of God" (Romans 8:22-24). Amen.

The Apostolic

Doug Schneider

We declare today Father, that we are partakers of the heavenly calling, a Kingdom that is not of this world but does belong in it (Hebrews 3:1). We thank You for sending Jesus Christ the Apostle and High Priest of our profession to this nation of Canada (Hebrews 3:1). Throughout our land today we 'consider' Your Son as a 'sent one' to us. We honour Him for laying down His life as a seed in the ground, so that multiplied other apostolic leaders would rise up as fruit of His ascended life. We recognize that years ago You sent different people groups to Canada to found it, frame it and facilitate the desires of Your heart. We recognize that our nation rests on the apostolic foundation of Jesus Christ and His righteous precepts. We declare that there is no other foundation than this, and that it's both sure and steadfast (1 Corinthians 3:11). Knowing the unique call that rests upon the Dominion of Canada at this hour of history, we join our voices with clarity and unity and cry out for the spirit of the apostolic to be released - true fathers and mothers have sown into, and now sow out, our sons and daughters of the Kingdom. Under the leadership of our Chief Apostle the Lord Jesus Christ, we commission and release with blessing 'the sent ones' into all spheres of regional, national and international society. We decree that you will succeed in all that the Father has purposed, that by Jesus Christ we might reconcile all things unto Himself; whether they be things in earth or in Heaven (Colossians 1:20). We speak into the spirit world today and say, "Let the apostolic men and women arise and establish Your Kingdom among us." Let apostles and apostolic centers be functioning with humility of character and supernatural gifting, and united with all other members of the Body of Christ. We give thanks today for Your manifold wisdom that is so easily seen in Your Church (Ephesians 3:10-11), and so powerfully released in Your Kingdom. Amen.

The Prophetic

Faytene Grasseschi

Lord, we acknowledge Your Word that tells us you have given prophets to Your Church to equip us and help bring us to maturity (Ephesians 4:13). We thank You for giving these men and women as gifts to us. We declare that we desire to receive them with wholeness of heart. Lord, we repent before You now on behalf of ourselves and our forefathers for any time in our history as a nation where we have not received the prophets, or prophetic voices, You have sent to us. For this we are deeply repentant. We recognize that we have grieved Your heart. As we have rejected them we have rejected You, the One who sent them. Father forgive us and cleanse us of this sin in our nation. Lord, You said in Your Word that if we received a prophet in the name of a prophet we would receive a prophet's reward (Matthew 10:41). We desire everything You have to give to us Lord. With this in mind, we declare today, that Canada is receiving the prophets that You are sending and therefore receiving a reward! We loose receptive hearts all across this land in the name of Jesus.

We declare that even those denominations and streams which, in the past, have not been receptive to Your prophets, and prophetic sent ones, are now responding with open hearts in the name of Jesus. We call forth the prophets of Canada to arise and take their place in humility, power and clarity. We declare they are being trained by the Spirit. We declare that they are releasing Your Word with clarity and releasing it in Your way. We trust You to teach them and instruct them well. We choose now to receive them in whatever 'package' You send them in. We also declare that the Church in Canada is receiving fresh ears to hear what the Spirit is saying (Revelation 2:29). We declare that true prophetic words from generations past are being discovered, dusted off, received, believed, contented for and birthed right on time. Let the Word of the Lord rattle in Your Church across this nation just as the valley of dry bones did before Ezekiel's eyes (Ezekiel 37:7). Thank You Lord! We declare, in the power of the Spirit, that prophets are coming out of the caves in Canada. We decree that they are arising from sea to sea and that they are loosing the Word of the Lord effectively across the land and even into other nations. We declare they are being released, and received, even now. Thank You Lord!

Houses of Prayer

Patricia Bootsma

"In that day 'I will restore David's fallen shelter—I will repair its broken walls and restore its ruins—and will rebuild it as it used to be.'" (Amos 9:11)

So "that the rest of mankind may seek the Lord..." (Act 15:17)

Father, we decree as Canadians that You are raising up the spirit, values and principles of the Tabernacle of David in our nation. In every province and territory we join with Heaven's model of worship (harp) and intercession (bowl) arising as incense before You perpetually and persistently (Revelation 5:8). We declare that the Bride of Christ is arising in Canada with a passionate heart of lovesick desire to come corporately to meet with You and cry out as one voice, "Come Lord Jesus, come" (Rev. 22:17). We declare in song and in prayer that God's power is being released into our nation. We decree that musicians, singers and intercessors are hearing the sounds of Heaven to be watchmen on the wall (Ezekiel 33:7). The house of the Lord in Canada will be a house of prayer (Matthew 21:13) and joyfully we come to agree with who You are in worship and what You want to do in intercession. We decree that Church leaders all across Canada are seeing with clear revelation the call to establish, encourage and support houses of prayer and that this is catching on like holy fire across the nation. We call forth full-time labourers for each house of prayer. We declare they will be released and resourced to effectively step into their post. We call forth houses of prayer for every city, region and sphere across Canada. We decree the house of prayer movement is helping to fuel the release of the great end time harvest of souls. We strike the ground with our cries to Heaven and salvation springs up from the ground in Canada (Isaiah 45:8). In Jesus' mighty name, the incense of worship and prayer is exalting and enthroning the Lord in Canada and enlisting Your help in the release of Your power and purposes in our nation.

The Economy

Femi & Remi Ogunrinde

Father, in the precious name of our Lord Jesus, we thank You for this great country. We uphold those in positions of trust and responsibilities over our economy. We acknowledge that it is neither our power nor the might of our hands that has gotten us the wealth we enjoy as a Nation. On the contrary, it is You that has given us the power to get wealth, that You may be able to establish Your covenant through this nation to be a blessing to other nations of the earth (Deuteronomy 8:18). Therefore we declare and decree over our nation's economic handlers, from our Prime Minister to the Ministers of Finance, Industry, Trade and other related government positions, that they are surrounded by men and women who are attentive to godly counsel and wisdom regarding how to steward our economy. We declare and decree over our nation that You shall have dominion from sea to sea, and from the river unto the ends of the earth (Psalm 72:8). We decree that our nation is blessed because You O God are our Lord (Psalm

33:12). We therefore declare Your blessings, Your refuge and prosperity over Canada - the strong and free. We declare that Your people shall dwell in safety in this land and we will prosper abundantly (Deuteronomy 33:28). Lord, we ask that You would restrain greed and financial recklessness in our nation. We call on You to remove every spirit of greed, ungodly speculation and financial recklessness in every facet of the economic life of this country. We pray that the Lord will grant wisdom and entrepreneurial spirit to the marketplace leaders, both young and old, in our country for innovation, inventions and entrepreneurship. We declare that Canada is rising as an innovative and economic leader globally and therefore able to bring support to other nations in times of need. As a nation we are supernaturally blessed and will be a blessing in Jesus' name!

The Government

Rob & Fran Parker

Intro: The Peace Tower stands impressively at the entrance to our Parliament, a structure easily recognised by all Canadians. What may not be readily noticed are the verses of Scripture carved in each of the three arches. These are verses that Solomon wrote nearly 3,000 years ago. The following decrees are written based on each of these scriptures.

South Arch: "Give the King thy Judgements O God and thy Righteousness Unto thy King's Son." (Psalm 72:1, KJV)

"Righteousness and justice are the foundation of Your throne..." O God (Psalm 89:14). Father, we recognize that Your throne is above the earth and we honour You as our King. Let our governments become an extension of Your justice and love for our fellow man restraining wrongdoing and promoting a just social order. Thank You for the generations who came before us who have stewarded Your precepts and now may Your Name continue to be honoured in today's governmental leaders.

East Arch: "He shall have dominion also from sea to sea and from the river to the ends of the earth." (Psalm 72:8, KJV)

Father we pray for Your dominion in the hearts of all Canadians, that Your Laws which are above man's laws would be increasingly preeminent in our land. We pray for a change in the hearts of our leaders that Your dominion would be seen in the value of life for all Canadians, including the unborn. We ask that our governments would uphold fairness and equality of all men before God and that they would protect the right of freedom of religion for all peoples.

West Arch: "Where there is no vision the people perish," (Proverbs 29:18, KJV) or, "Where there is no prophetic revelation, the people cast off restraint" (Proverbs 29:18, ESV).

Keep us from temptation, oh God, by helping us to keep our vision ever on You. We ask that You would help us to bring revelation in the service of Your Kingdom come and that people would see genuine love for others through us. Keep our government officials from self-seeking agendas and let them truly be Your 'servants' as described in Your Word (Romans 13:4). Let those Members of Parliament and Senators who know You and love You become a great unified light shining in the halls and offices of our Parliament bringing revelation of Jesus as the King of Kings, Lord of Lords, and the One who holds government on His shoulders (Isaiah 9:6).

The Military

Rob & Fran Parker

"The centurion replied, 'Lord, I do not deserve to have You come under my roof. But just say the word, and my servant will be healed. For I myself am a man under authority, with soldiers under me. I tell this one, 'Go,' and he goes; and that one, 'Come,' and he comes. I say to my servant, 'Do this,' and he does it.' When Jesus heard this, He was astonished and said to those following Him, 'I tell you the truth, I have not found anyone in Israel with such great faith.'" (Matthew 8:8-10)

"Greater love has no one than this, that he lay down his life for his friends." (John 15:13)

Intro: These two passages speak precisely into the spiritual roots and challenges of our Canadian Armed Forces. The Centurion understood both the meaning of authority, and the power of Jesus Christ. Our men and women in uniform are the same; they serve under authority, and exercise authority over others. We pray that they will have a revelation of the living Word and bread of life (John 6:35), and recognize the power of Jesus Christ. They exercise this authority in the name of the Canadian people. We elect a government, that government exercises authority over the Armed Forces. Pray that our government will wield this authority, this power, righteously.

Canada has not fought a war on its own soil for over a hundred years. We are secure here in our nation. We send soldiers overseas to help others in their struggles. Whether to the titanic struggles of the World Wars, to peacekeeping operations, Canada, and by extension her soldiers, volunteer to lay down their lives for their (Canada's) friends. These revelations are an excellent guide for our prayers.

Prayer: Father, we pray for wisdom for the leaders of the Canadian Armed Forces. We pray that our political leaders will send our men and women into harm's way only for righteous reasons, guided by the wisdom of Holy Spirit. We pray that our military leaders, at all levels, will be guided by Holy Spirit in all they do, using the great authority vested in them righteously and for the good.

Lord, we pray for honour. We pray that the people and the government of Canada will recognize the sacrifice and the love that our men and women in uniform represent. We pray that their wounds (physical or spiritual) will be cared for properly and that Canadians will honour them and their families. Father we pray for our military families. We recognize that they too are subject to authority and make great sacrifices in Canada's name. We pray that they will be properly cared for. We pray that spouses will kindle the fires of the home during the absence of military members - even through multiple moves and changes in postings. We pray that children will not suffer through the long absences of their parents and that, by God's grace, military marriages will be preserved and strengthened through long periods of absence.

The Media

Faytene Grasseschi

Father we thank You for the gift of media which has the power to disciple our nation (Matthew 28:19). Because of this, we bring Canada's media, in all its forms, before You now. In Jesus' name we decree a massive infusion of the glory, power, presence and truth of God into every aspect of media in Canada. We ask that You would shake everything that can be shaken in Canadian media so that only that which can not be shaken will remain (Hebrews 12:27). We call forth Your voice to be mighty in Canadian media in the name of Jesus (Psalm 29:3). We declare that You are mighty to save (Zephaniah 3:17). We therefore pray for the salvation of every person in our nation connected with the media sphere. We loose revelation unto salvation over news anchors, writers, editors, reporters, executives, financiers, graphic designers, producers and all others connecting with Canada's media. We ask for a mighty visitation of Your Spirit upon them now in Jesus' name. Where unrighteous messages have been perpetuated through Canada's media we now loose the conviction of the Holy Spirit - clean house we pray in Jesus' name. We also declare that all networks which produce and perpetuate pornography or other defiling content are being swiftly restrained in Jesus' name. We declare righteousness in the CRTC and that they are only approving those networks which will contribute positively to the moral fabric of Canada and that they are revoking licenses of those who do not. We bless Christian media to expand and become the most watched and best produced media in our nation! We loose skill, finances and viewership favour over all those producing righteous media in Jesus' name. We declare the media is becoming a mass harvest tool to bring many to salvation and to teach Canada in the ways of the Lord. We call forth a new generation of revivalists, reformers, righteous activists and entertainers in the spirit of holiness through media. We declare massive favour on these ones now. We also declare that tax payer dollars being given to biased or unrighteous media production is being revoked in the Jesus' name and being re-directed to those who will stand for Godly values and truth. In Jesus' name, we decree that the media in Canada is releasing the voice of the Lord and no other. Father brood over the media in Canada and release the revelation of Your Son through it we pray.

Education

Faytene Grasseschi

Father we bring our educational system and educators before You now in the mighty name of Jesus. Your Word declares that if we train up a child in the way they should go that when they are old they will not depart from it (Proverbs 22:6). We therefore acknowledge how important Canada's education is. It can influence a person even into their adult years. We pray for the spirit of sanctification in the Canadian educational system from sea to sea. We thank You for the righteous heritage that many of our schools and universities have. We thank You that many of them were dedicated to You at the foundation and that many of the founders desired to teach pupils the Word of God. Father remember these dedications and raise up a movement of righteousness through the educational system. We decree that this movement will impact our entire nation! We pray for all teachers, administrators, assistants, legislators, curriculum writers and any others who have influence over what is taught to our children. We loose the revelation of Jesus Christ over them now. We pray that those who do not know You would be drawn to salvation, filled with Holy Spirit and used to train the next generation in excellence and righteousness. We speak to any ungodly curriculum that is currently woven into any of our school systems. We declare it is being swiftly removed and replaced with teaching that honours Your heart and ways. We loose the spirit of revival into our schools and campuses from sea to sea. We call forth visitations of Holy Spirit in classrooms and that students would be raised up to host moves of Your Spirit in power. We call forth signs and wonders on the campuses and mass moves of salvation. Lord, we dedicate our educational system to You and ask that You would fill it with Your glory. Raise it up to set a standard for the nations of the Earth, we pray.

Jewish People in Canada

Peg Byars

By the eternal command of God and in the mighty name of
Yeshua, the Messiah, we pray and declare:

> "The Lord bless you and keep you; the Lord
> make His face shine upon you, and be gracious
> to you; the Lord lift up His countenance upon
> you, and give you peace" (Numbers 6:24-26).

We join our hearts together and thank You Father for
allowing Canada to be a safe place of refuge for Your
Jewish people for many years. We bless and thank You for
the significant contributions they have made to this nation.
We thank You, Shepherd of Israel, that in these years of
their scattering, You have prepared their true homeland for
them – the reborn State of Israel. As Canadian believers,
we take heed to Your Word from Jeremiah 31:10 which
says:

Hear the word of the Lord, O nations,

And declare it in the isles afar off, and say:

"He who scattered Israel will gather him

And keep him as a shepherd does his flock."

Awake, precious ones in the Canadian diaspora - hear and obey – your Redeemer declares that it is time to come home, and so we boldly declare God's promise: "Fear not, for I AM with you . . . I WILL gather you from the west . . ." (Isaiah 43:5, KJV). We ask You Lord for a spiritual awakening within the believing community in our nation, to know that we have a divine calling and mandate to bless Israel (Genesis 12:3), to comfort Your people (Isaiah 40:1), to serve them (Isaiah 14:1-2), and to carry them home (Isaiah 49:22). Awaken us to know that we will be held accountable before You for how we respond to Your Word. Raise up a company in Canada to help Your people home and to bless and support the Canadian aliyah[2] ministries that You have called into service, for such a time as this. In Yeshua's all-powerful name, we repent on behalf of our nation for any anti-Semitic, anti-Israel, anti-Christ spirit that would want to harass and persecute the Jews in Canada. We pray for the yoke of the enemy to be broken off all those who carry this spirit so that they too may receive the gift of redemption available to them through the shed blood of the one and only Messiah. We thank You Father, that as shaking takes place, You are speaking to the hearts of Your Jewish people – "Return to Me and I will return to you" (Nehemiah 1:9; Isaiah 44:22; Zechariah 1:3). Father God, by Your grace and our obedience, may there be a mighty remnant of believing followers of Yeshua from the nation of Canada who will be counted worthy to go up each year to Jerusalem in the days to come, to worship the King of the Jews at the Feast of Tabernacles! (Zechariah 14:16-17, Isaiah 2:1-4). Lord, as we align ourselves with Your sovereign plan for Israel and the nations, let Your rain and Your reign be upon Canada! We pray for the Peace of Jerusalem (Psalm 122:6).

First Peoples & Métis

Faytene Grasseschi

Father, thank You for the First Peoples and Métis peoples of Canada. We acknowledge the tremendous gift You have given them of spiritual authority, sensitivity, intuition to care for the land, respect for the generations and much more. We honour and acknowledge that You, in Your sovereign will, gave them the original stewardship of this land which is now called Canada. We also acknowledge that the gift of stewardship, and leadership, that You gave them was not only for past generations but meant to be a blessing for the current one, and future ones, as well. We ask that You would empower them to be all that You have sovereignly ordained them to be. We also loose a fresh wave of healing and unity throughout Canada. We ask that You would move by Your Spirit to empower indigenous leaders to walk together with each other in unity and righteousness, and to walk with non-indigenous leaders, for the welfare of future generations. Lord, we continue to humble ourselves on behalf of our nation and repent for the ways that non-indigenous Canadians have participated in exploiting, hurting or defiling the First Peoples or Métis in any way. Father, we desperately beseech You to continue to heal these wounds in our nation. Thank You for the healing that has taken place in recent years as the Canadian government openly apologized to the indigenous peoples of Canada, and, as they have released forgiveness. We rejoice in this forward progress and declare that You who began a good work will bring it to completion (Philippians 1:6). Lord, we loose a fresh wave of Your Holy Spirit to encounter all of the First Peoples, and Métis, in our nation. We pray this for every generation, from the elders to the nursing babes. We call forth a fresh wave of healing, restoration, resurrection power, signs and wonders and a mighty move of Your Spirit. Draw multitudes to Yourself. We pray You would raise them up as a voice for Your glory in Canada. Use them to be a voice for righteousness and genuine justice we pray. Restore them as gatekeepers in the land to resist darkness and loose Your glorious light. We call them forth into the fullness of their calling in You (Ephesians 1:18) and declare that they will arise and bear great fruit, and that fruit will remain (John 15:16). We thank You for the First Peoples and Métis of Canada. Father, would You be gracious to them, cause Your face to shine upon them and grant them great peace (Numbers 6:25).

Inuit

Bill Prankard

In the powerful name of Jesus we pray and decree:

Blessing and prosperity for every Inuit community, family and individual. We speak honour to the elders whose wisdom and leadership have preserved Inuit culture and have set a righteous example to future generations. We ask for Your mantle of wise leadership to rest powerfully on Inuit government representatives, educators and spiritual leaders. Give them courage to stand for godly principles in the face of changing values. We call forth the gatekeepers of the north to rise up in the anointing of the Holy Spirit, to take their rightful place and lead their people back to God. We raise a standard of the Spirit against every destructive force assailed against our First Peoples. We declare that the epidemic of suicide among Inuit youth shall be stopped; that they shall be set free from the chains and bondage of alcohol, drugs and abuse. We say to the north, "Give them up!" (Isaiah 43:6). Heal broken hearts; restore fractured families; reveal Your love to those who are forgotten and lonely. Holy Spirit, we ask You to infuse this restored, renewed and revived generation with Your anointing. Fulfill Your eternal purpose in them and thrust them forth into the whitened harvest field (Matthew 9:38). We declare that they shall become carriers of the fire of God, and that it will ignite and spread to every Arctic community. May Canada's North experience a mighty move of God that will set an example to the nation and to the world. We say to Canada's Inuit, "You are the true north strong and free!"

From The River To The Ends Of The Earth

(Reflection Regarding Francophone Canada)

Alain Caron

I often think of the arrival of my French ancestors in Canada. I can picture their boats appearing at the entrance of the Saint-Lawrence, that great river that opens the way to the heart of our nation. I don't know all the dreams that were in their hearts when they arrived. They called the land the 'New World.' Some came to find a passage to richer lands, others just hoped for a favourable place to start a new life, others to escape religious persecution, while some others just signed on for the adventure. I've read there was sense of mission among them to bring the gospel to the inhabitants of this land, the First Nations.

I often think of the way this was done, and the fruits that are with us today. I see the pain in the heart of the First Peoples around us; I see the pride of my own people, the

French Canadians, and the need we ourselves have for the gospel now.

If only we had come with more humility and respect, presenting the gospel like a treasure we wanted to share; if only we had asked if we could seek the Father together, and learned from each other with open hearts.

And I think about what the Book we brought with us says:

> Remember therefore from where you have fallen;
> repent and do the first works.
> (Rev. 2:5 NKJV)

We need to go back. We need to humble ourselves and ask the original people if we can seek the ways of the Lord Yeshua together.

If we want the Great River to truly become the point of penetration for the gospel in this land, and if we ever want to see its glorious message reach to the ends of the earth, it will have to reach the depths of our hearts first (Psalm 72:8). Then we will truly enter in the 'New World' - together. I pray for that with my whole heart.

Francophone Canada

Faytene Grasseschi

Father, thank You for Quebec and the Francophone people of Canada. We honour the Founding Fathers of our nation who came from France, many of them because they felt a personal call from You to advance the Gospel of Jesus Christ here. We honour them as some of Canada's finest pioneers and revivalists. Father, we pray that You would blow afresh on the coals of revival all throughout Quebec and French speaking Canada. We call forth a mighty move of Holy Spirit to draw them to You and set them so ablaze that they begin to loose revival fire all across Canada and to the ends of the earth. As Quebec has been used as a forerunner on moral issues in the past, we call them forth to be forerunners of righteousness in this generation. We speak to the seeds of righteous reformation and ask that You would cause them to spring forth in power for Your glory. We pray for the youth of Quebec. We speak to the spirit of suicide and immorality and declare that it is being overtaken by the spirit of life and purity in Christ Jesus. We call forth a mighty youth and young adult awakening in

Quebec in Jesus name. We call forth righteous revivalists and reformers in every sphere of Francophone Canadian society: in media, education, government, business, the arts and more. We also pray for harvesters to be loosed into this harvest field (Matthew 9:38). God we ask that even now You would call missionaries from across Canada and the world to come and sow in prayer and proclamation of the gospel to French speaking Canada once again. We pray for the older generation to be awakened to the love and goodness of God and salvation through Jesus. We speak to the immigrant community in Quebec and loose revival fires to hit that community as well. Set them ablaze for Your glory Jesus. Finally Lord, we pray that You would heal all outstanding wounds between French Canada and English Canada. Raise up ministers of reconciliation in the Church, and in government, to lead the way in this reconciliation we pray. We ask for a great healing of our land that would lead to a massive advancement of the Gospel of Jesus Christ and would be an example to the nations of the world. We honour and bless Quebec and French speaking Canada in the name of Jesus. We cut off every negative word that has been spoken against them and call forth the blessing of Your fullness and glory to come to them in Jesus' name.

The Nations Here

Peggy Kennedy

Lord, You have formed a place called Canada. From the earliest times this land has been the home of many nations, our First Peoples. Throughout our history You have gathered many people to this place in successive waves of arrival to these shores. Truly, it is the work of Your hands that Canada is today a community of nations. You have gathered anointings from many nations to come to this place. By Your grace in a spirit of partnership, we declare that You will cause those anointings to mingle and that Your purposes for global harvest will be advanced in and through our land. Cause our hearts to be opened to see the great opportunity we have as Canada to meet and embrace one another in our unique ways of carrying Your Presence. Let our voices now blend in praise to You. Let us now find, in our many languages, a harmony of worship, intercession, and spiritual agreement. We declare that You will not be denied a harvest in our nation. "All the families of the nations will bow down before You for dominion belongs to the Lord" (Psalm 22:27-28).   Our eyes are upon You to release an empowering grace into our partnership so that we will be formed by Your hand into a rising force that will carry Your Name to the ends of the Earth.

Relationship with Israel

Giulio Lorefice Gabeli

Thank You Lord for our nation of Canada and the righteous foundation of God's Word that has shaped the very core fabric of our government, the law, and the infrastructure of our society. Thank You for the Judaeo-Christian values that has made our nation strong and prosperous! May our leaders never forget that our history as a nation was rooted in the value systems of God's revelation to the Jewish people and that they are the apple of His eye (Zechariah 2:8). May they be reminded that in blessing Israel; we will be blessed as a nation (Genesis 12:3). We loose courage over them to confront every anti-semitic challenge, finger pointing and hatred towards the Jewish people and the State of Israel. May our nation's leaders stand with Israel even against the negative tide of anti-Zionism within the United Nations forum. May they have the courage to expose the lies and confront the false propaganda being disseminated in and through anti-Semetic media that seeks to discredit the legitimacy of the State of Israel. We declare that our leaders never capitulate to international pressure from oil rich Middle Eastern nations that desire to see Israel destroyed. We pray our government leaders will have the moral fortitude to stand and defend Israel and the Jewish people even when it costs us economically and the loss of political allies. We loose courage over our leaders to declare that the city of Jerusalem is the undivided capital of the Jewish State of Israel and the courage to lead the way by moving our embassy to the city of Jerusalem. Lord we declare that Canada's relationship with Israel and the Jewish people will be a model for other nations to follow and emulate. Thank You Lord that our nation will be blessed and highly favoured politically, economically and financially because of our relationship to Israel! Thank You Lord that Canada will continue to be spared from devastating and destructive natural disasters and plagues because He who watches over Israel neither slumbers nor sleeps (Psalm 121:4) and You will do the same for Canada! Lord, we declare that Canada and Israel will forge a greater bond of unity and friendship that will be the marvel of the nations of the world in these end times. May the shalom of God overwhelm the nation of Canada and Israel despite any international turmoil and trouble. We decree that Your promises will prevail over both nations.

Healing to the Nations

Brent Sloss

Thank You Father for the Body of Christ in Canada walking in the fullness of the healing love and power of Jesus. We call the Canadian Church to rise and be healed and to walk in its destiny to heal and restore the nations to Christ. We declare that the Canadian Church walks in the supernatural gift to be all things to all people in every ethnic group, and win many (1 Corinthians 9:22). We call forth the gift of reconciliation to flow into the nations from our hands and lives, healing even ancient wounds of unforgiveness, offence, division and hatred. We call forth new waves of peace-making, humble and dynamic servant-missionaries to be raised and sent to every people group in every nation, establishing and multiplying the Kingdom of Jesus in every place. Canada, we call you into your divine purpose as healer of the nations (Revelation 22:2)! Lord, we declare that Canada will be a father nation to many other nations helping them move into the fullness of their calling! Lord, we thank You that Canada will truly bring healing to many nations that are fatherless spiritually!

Lord, we declare that the Canadian Church will lead the way in modelling what it means to walk together as fathers and sons preparing the way for the King of Glory to return! Lord, thank You that many are hearing the call in this hour! Amen!

Prophetic Expectation

Peggy Kennedy

Father, we have heard Your voice declaring Your heart, longing, and prophetic intention for our nation of Canada. We repent when we have not treasured these words to the full measure of their fulfillment. Forgive us for allowing the words to be plucked from the pathway of our hearts. We declare that Your words and intentions for our land are good. We declare that You are tilling the soil of our hearts to receive, cherish and allow these seeds of Your prophetic desires to be well-tended and bring forth the full potential. There are many coast to coast to coast who have received the prophetic words with joy. Strengthen us so that we continue in joyful expectation that the words will be fulfilled. You are increasing the capacity of Your people so that these words will not wither in the shallow soil of our lives. Let these words penetrate deeply into our spirits. Lord, we repent for times that as Your Church we have been easily distracted. We acknowledge that at times waiting for the fulfillment has caused us to doubt Your

Word or doubt that You had the power to fulfill it. We invite Your Spirit to search us and root out the thorns of unbelief, life's worries, riches, and pleasures that have choked out what You desire (Matthew 13:1-23). We declare that Your words of prophetic destiny over our nation will be fulfilled and will not be held back. Let our hearts be noble and good hearts to hear Your prophetic word over Canada, retain it, and by persevering see the crop come forth (Galatians 6:9). There will be a harvest of what You have faithfully sown. We will not cast away our confidence (Hebrews 10:35). Thank You for releasing grace to sustain our eager expectation that You will fulfill Your promises to the nation of Canada.

Prophecies for Canada

(By Recognized Prophetic Ministries)

Puritan Reformers, 1776

The Light And Glory by Peter Marshall records a 1776 prophecy for Canada:

"Around 1776 this prophecy was given by the Puritan Reformers, when the British Empire Loyalists turned north to settle in Canada in order to remain under British rule. When zealous Americans sought to persecute them because of this decision, the Spirit of the Lord spoke through their prophets saying, 'Do not hinder these people. Let them move to Canada. Do not seek to incorporate the land of Canada into America. I am in the independence of America from Britain, and will mightily use this country. But Canada has been reserved by me for the Last Days for a special work.'"

> "CANADA HAS BEEN RESERVED BY ME FOR THE LAST DAYS FOR A SPECIAL WORK."

Could this prophecy, delivered over 200 years ago, be a confirmation of a prophetic word concerning Canada delivered by Dr. David Yonggi Cho, of Seoul, Korea in 1975 and 1984? - James Watt (a Canadian called to call Canadian Christians to intercede for their country)."[3]

Dr. Yonggi Cho, 1975 & 1984

Evangel Tabernacle, Kelowna, BC, 1975

"When I came to Canada, the Holy Spirit spoke in my heart, 'Son, you have come to the place which I chose. This country is the country I chose to fill the gap.'

Being a Canadian is now a welcome hallmark throughout the whole world...You have the welcome open door like the Philadelphia Church in Revelation. You have the

> "RISE UP, CANADA!...GOD IS DEPENDING ON YOU."

finances, well-trained personnel, and a good Church. God calls you to rise up to meet this challenge before Christ comes. A clear-cut clarion trumpet sound is coming to Canada. Rise up, Canada! God wants your young men and women to rise up and give their lives as living sacrifices. God needs your money, your businesses, your homes, your lives to be dedicated to Him...God is depending upon you....I know that you will do it."[4]

Sackville, Nova Scotia, 1984

At a Church growth seminar, Dr. Yonggi Cho reiterated the earlier prophecy, and adding to it:

"Five years ago I visited Canada and traveled from Montreal to Vancouver by car. I was preaching from town to town, and while I was speaking I felt somewhat depressed. The Canadian church seemed so small.

But wherever I went, the Holy Spirit spoke in my heart that God was going to raise up tremendous churches in Canada and that Canada would be used as a missionary sending country, and that Canada would open the way for Jesus Christ to return to this earth.

> ## "GOD IS GOING TO BLESS CANADA AND THE CANADIAN CHURCH IS GOING TO RISE UP ONCE AGAIN TO GO TO THE FOUR CORNERS OF THE WORLD."

I was afraid to confess that, but when I was praying....the Spirit of the Lord would impress my heart to say it. I was afraid because I already thought that America was far greater than Canada. If ever God would use a country. He would use America instead of Canada...But again and again God spoke to my heart that He was going to use Canada. So finally in Toronto...I prophesied as the Holy Spirit anointed me. I really believe that God is going to bless Canada and the Canadian Church is going to rise up once again and go to the four corners of the world and bring the gospel of Jesus Christ to pave the way for His second coming."

(The magnitude of recent Canadian missionary and church planting endeavors and the outpouring of the Spirit, which began at the Airport Vineyard and is touching every nation in the world, could represent the beginning of the fulfillment of Dr. Yonggi Cho's prophecies.)[5]

Smith Wigglesworth & Charles S. Price:

"Though this account cannot be substantiated by documentation, it is relayed by James Watt who was one of the leaders in Latter Rain Revival in North Battleford Saskatchewan, 1948 -1953.

In the 1920's Smith Wigglesworth and Dr. Charles S. Price foretold of a significant revival in Northern Canada in the late 40's. They described it as a great wave of blessing that would bring great hope to the world but, because man would introduce a mixture, God in grief would withdraw. The wave would secede, leaving a desert condition for a generation of 50 years. But at the end of the century, another wave would roll in, 10 times more the power and glory of the first. It would continue in blessing until the return of the King!"[6]

Jim Watt, 2006

(Of the Latter Rain Revival)

"God said, 'This is a thing I have started already and is even now progressing. I will pour out My Spirit and wild fire will rush across Canada. Canada has had revival,' He said, 'You've seen that. But,' He said, 'I want to tell you that is nothing to what I am about to do,' He said, 'It will be 100 times, a 1000 times, greater than all past revivals put together...Canadians are not feared. It's just that Canada is God's for the Last Days in a very special way and the United States can work with Canada in this but they can't duplicate what Canadians can do."[7]

Alistar Petrie, 2006

"God, years ago, said to many saintly people in Canada, 'The time would come when a revival will come to your land that will be 100 times more powerful than all the historical revivals, to this date, put together.....healing reconciliation and destiny are very clearly the hallmarks of why this nation exists on behalf of all the other nations of the world."[8]

Chief Kenny Blacksmith, 2006

"In my dream we were in a boat going across the lake and I remember we were coming to a peninsula ahead of us, and, on this peninsula I saw the different types of tee-pees and sweat lodges and long houses. I mean, they were all types of lodges of First Nations Peoples. I remember as I got closer I could hear them shouting, 'Hurry, hurry, for it's going to cover you.' And I remember just looking to the corner of my eye on both sides and I literally saw this white light and I looked around me and all I saw was this wave of pure white light...but this wave of light just kept sweeping the land and it covered them as they were running and it covered the hills and the valleys. It covered the whole land. Later on the Word of the Lord came in Ezekiel that the wave of the presence of the glory of God, the glory of God is going to sweep this land."[9]

James Arreak (Inuit), 2006

"People began to have visions, dreams about these old dams or huge rocks. Solid, frozen, cold rocks. Stones. And these rocks that that had kept the Holy Spirit from flowing were being forced into...this giant river was coming upon them and as the river hit them they began to splinter, they began to break up and what seemed solid, what seemed right, what seemed unmovable was totally shaken and removed...I believe this is what God is about to do in this nation. This is why I believe we're having tremendous visions and great dreams of visions of rivers coming on this nation...and the First Nations are having these dreams as well....I believe we are at the verge of this thing."[10]

David Mainse, 2006

"I have great hope for government in Canada because government is established by God. God's purposes, God's plan for Canada will be fulfilled."[11]

Stacey Campbell, 2006

"If you look in the history of Canada, Canada has always had a call to the nations. Whenever God has birthed something here in the spirit it has never just remained here in Canada."[12]

Cindy Jacobs, 2004

"God is going to change the economy of Canada. One day, Canada will so blessed that she will lend to many nations and not borrow. And some times you think, 'Wow, how could that ever happen?' But with God nothing is impossible. I prophesied last night that there would be a time when the Canadian dollar would be worth more than the US dollar. That is mind boggling. And I said, 'You don't need to say it was just a Canadian dollar anymore because Canadian dollars are good dollars. And we know that God is going to do something very special. The Lord has been speaking to us about farmers. This is dairy farmers, beef farmers, wheat farmers, all kinds of farmers and it is a time to pray for the farmers of Canada - and the fishermen and women, the fisheries, and the fishing boats. God wants to bring a blessing on the land. Biblically, the Bible says if you are willing and obedient you will eat the good of the land, meaning the land is good!...You are going to send relief all over the world. Canada will feed the poor and be the breadbasket that will send out all kinds of relief across the nations of the earth. Well if that's going to happen then you have to have money to do it...Canada is the only nation in the world with a leaf on her flag and so Canada is called to heal nations. Revelation 22 says, 'The leaves on the tree of life are for the healing of the nations,' and so God has brought many many nations here and these nations are going to change other nations."

Rachel Hickson, March 2001

"Oh Canada, oh Canada, oh Canada. I see your flag with its two bands of red - it is one of the most striking flags in the world. I see the two strikes of red - coast to coast. God is going to paint the blood of His precious Son Jesus from the north to the south, from the west to the east. And that white no-man's land is a cry for holiness...There are different fires that the Lord is kindling. A maple leaf in the fall months is ablaze with fire red colour. Your nation is being raised as one who will bring healing to the nations.

God is going to take off of this land passivity and the false peace you've preached. He will again make you a true reconciler and a true leaf for healing of the nations. He will restore your diplomatic status and it will be a true diplomacy that stands for integrity and righteousness and that brings together that which has been torn apart. I feel that what's been going on with the reconciliation with the Jewish People, God is going to use you as a reconciler just as Norway has been recognized in Europe, I believe you will be recognized as reconcilers in the world. And Norway and you are going to come together and do something in the Middle East. I just feel these things and if I were going to prophesy anything about Canada, it would be this; this is what I am feeling in my spirit at this time...

Something is happening in your land, Canada. But you must have ears to hear what the Spirit is saying and I believe the first place to start is with lots of tears. God wants to get you connected with your land again. He wants you to become unashamedly Canadian! Put Canada back in your heart. It doesn't matter whether your passport says you're Canadian or not, if you are living here you have a responsibility to let this land become part of you. You've got to carry the land in your heart."

Cindy Jacobs, 2004

"'In My sovereign purposes this nation was not birthed in a revolution. But yet, within the hearts of My people there is a time that I am bringing you to,' says God, 'where in your hearts I am planting a revolution. And I would say to you, it is time to arise! It is time to stand up and fight for lo the enemy is at your door,' says God, 'The enemy is knocking and the enemy has designs upon this nation. Not just from one place, but even,' the Lord says, 'there are giants in this land but they are coming from other lands,' says the Lord.

> "I AM RAISING UP THOSE WHO ARE ACTIVISTS...I AM RAISING UP A NEW BREED OF CANADIANS."

'And they desire to take over the foundations of this nation. But I would say to you, I am raising up those who love not their life unto death. I am raising up those who are activists, I am raising up those who will say, 'No, I will not allow this unrighteousness in my nation.' For I am raising up a new breed of Canadians,' says God, 'And even I am shifting this nation in a new direction. Look to see what I will do.' For the Lord says, 'if you will fast and pray, will I not even change the government, the leaders, the way this nation has been going.' The Lord says, 'I have big hands, and I see this nation slipping down and down. But will I not reach up and bear My mighty right arm and catch this nation in My everlasting arms,' says God, 'And will I not lift you up and will I not make you great among all the nations in the Earth? Hear the cry! Hear the cry for revolution, revolution from unrighteousness! Revolution from those who have designs upon the land I called you to take dominion of. For there is a dominion anointing I have given to My people. I am giving you authority and I will expand your authority,' says God, 'from sea to sea.' In 2005 there will be a massive change..." [13] [14]

Cindy Jacobs, March 2001

"Psalm 72:8,9,12-15, 'He shall have dominion from sea to sea. From the river to the ends of the earth. Those who dwell in the wilderness will bow before Him and His enemies will lick the dust.' And this is so powerful as you read this. 'He will deliver the needy when He cries, the poor also, him who has no helper. He will spare the poor and needy.' This is all prophetic for Canada. 'He will save the souls of the needy. He will redeem their life from oppression and violence. And precious shall be their blood in His sight.' And then verse 15. I want you to look at this, 'Prayer will also be made for Him continually.' That's day and night. 'And daily He shall be praised.'...

And the Holy Spirit just began to show me that Canada is coming to a place of her own anointing, and that there is a shift taking place even now...The Lord showed me clearly that during WW II when the Jews came in the S.S. Louis to the shores of Canada you turned away your destiny for a generation and because of that a judgment came on Canada, and in that time the giants increased in the land. Abortion came in; there is no longer prayer in schools everyday;

Bible reading, these things...And so it is my understanding that in public school now they do not begin everyday with the Lord's prayer any more, that it is not that way.

I want to say it again. Listen to me. You should pray that prayer in Psalm 73: 'He shall preserve you, and your children.' You need to be preserved from violence. I want to tell you something if you do not overthrow this and work to put prayer in schools you will have what we have had. The shooting outside of Calgary was only the beginning of sorrows. I pray that you hear this word, because we did some intercession even about this, I believe last year or the year before. And I feel I gave you a window of grace, but you have to understand that is not enough.

> ## "EVERY SCHOOL IN CANADA NEEDS TO BE COVERED IN INTERCESSION."

Every school in Canada needs to be covered in intercession. Every pastor at every church in every city needs to pray and have his intercessors pray everyday for the schools in their particular city. Amen? You have got to raise up watchmen on the wall. Please heed me. I want to tell you that there are no boundaries to this thing. The Bible says, 'believe the word of the prophets and you shall prosper.'

Let me tell you something. . .Prayer needs to be made both day and night. You need to stand up. And so the Lord wants to give you dominion from sea to sea. And not only that it says in verse 26, 'The court shall be seated and they shall take away his dominion to consume and destroy forever. Then the kingdom and the dominion and the greatness of the kingdoms under the whole earth shall be given to the people, the saints of the Most High. His Kingdom is an everlasting Kingdom and all dominion shall serve and obey Him.' It says, 'He shall have dominion from sea to sea and also to the ends of the earth.' It also says that in Zechariah 9...I believe the Holy Spirit has shown me several things. One is that I believe that you have come to Hebron in this nation. Hebron means 'alliance or union.'...Hebron was the first place that David ruled, but he didn't have Jerusalem yet. I believe you have reached a Hebron in this nation...

There is a 'Hebron' that has been released. All Right? And so we see that there was a rag tag band of men that became mighty in God and they became fighters. All Right? There's several things represented by Hebron. One is that it was in Hebron that Abram's name was changed to Abraham, father of nations (Genesis 17:5). And Sarah was called mother of nations. So what are you modeling here? You have come, and I believe what you did in this past year or so, maybe you didn't know what you were doing, but

> ## "GOD HAS RELEASED A FATHERING AND MOTHERING ANNOINTING THAT IS GOING TO BREAK BARRENESS OF THIS NATION."

God has changed the leaders in this nation from Abrams to Abrahams, from Sarai to Sarahs, and...God has released a fathering and a mothering anointing that is going to break barrenness off this nation and you are going to begin to see great fruit and great harvest. Amen? And you also know if you study it that - Hebron was the place that Abraham actually purchased. And this is a sign of covenant of God.

You see if you go back in the history of Canada you see there was a people that made a covenant with God for this nation. Amen? But what happened, was when you didn't go in...and take your destiny, which was actually to heal nations and shield the Jews and protect the Jews when they came to your shores...We see that you didn't go on in your destiny and you can be likened to this, because Hebron was a place where the twelve spies came. And they cut the cluster of grapes in Hebron. And so Caleb came out and said [to] Joshua, 'We're more than able to take this land.' And so the Lord shows me that there are those who have for many years believed that this land could be taken. They were the Caleb's waiting for this time to say, 'give me this mountain.' This is your hour. The Lord also showed me this there are prayers of your forefathers and mothers that God is getting ready to answer.

He is going to answer through you to re-establish justice and righteousness in this land. That there are those who have said the scripture, 'that He shall have dominion from sea to sea.' Those who gave that to this nation as a scripture for this nation. They not only gave it but they prayed it and believed it. And there is a time when we are going to mix together the anointing of the generations.

And God is saying, 'do I find a generation with faith that is saying, 'Let's go in and take this promised land.'' I believe you have come to Hebron, but it's time to go to Jerusalem. And you can see this Jerusalem in two ways. One, is that there is a physical Jerusalem, which is a governmental seat. And then you can see where Daniel 7 comes into play, that when you get the government, and the Spirit-filled Prime Minister, that I have prophesied. When that happens in this nation you will have your Jerusalem. Amen? God wants to do that for you, but you're going to have to fight for it, because there are mean spirits in this land that want to stop you in Hebron. Amen? Are you getting this? So in this land it is much harder now than it would have been before. Because there's a spirit of diversity and all these things

> **"GOD WANTS TO DO THAT FOR YOU, BUT YOU'RE GOING TO HAVE TO FIGHT FOR IT."**

have come in. And you know the Holy Spirit's been saying its about your mind. Isn't it? The pluralistic thinking has to go.

And the thinking of your forefathers and foremothers - you're going to have to come to the place where we're going to say that was God's will for this nation...And the Lord showed me a major key to this is going to be worship. See, Caleb was a Kenesite. He wasn't of the tribe of Judah, but he came with Judah. All Right? And he got the anointing of the tribe of Judah, because he married a woman from the tribe of Judah. The tribe of Judah,

> ## "THE LORD SHOWED ME A MAJOR KEY TO THIS IS GOING TO BE WORSHIP."

according to Psalm 60:7, was the law giver tribe. Judah shall be the lawgiver. Alright? So therefore you will release the law giving anointing through Judah in this land. Amen? It's not just any worship, listen to me, It's not just any worship. It's not enough to worship. You have to worship specifically. You have to get the mind of the Lord.

What do you want sung over this land? What voice should be heard over the land?

What will break open the heavens? What do you want to do and do that thing! Amen? Just like you pray specifically, you must praise specifically.

Because then you will split open the heavens. Amen? So this is something God showed us as a strategy. So God knows what He is up to and He's trying to mix this anointing here in Canada...why do you think you have this incredible worship coming out of Canada?

> ## "I HAVE BEEN WAITING FOR A NATION WHICH WOULD HAVE THE ANNOINTING TO HEAL ISAAC AND ISHMAEL."

The Lord wants you to rise to a new place. See you have come to Hebron. And now the Lord has showed me that you became fathers and mothers in the spirit and you took a hold of your destiny to go heal the nations. And that's why you are going to Israel, to Jerusalem...Canada, I prophesy to you. You have the anointing to break open this war...I want to tell you who can bring healing for this matter. It is Canada. And you must rise up Canada! And you must go! And you must fight and you must stand. And the Lord says, 'I have been waiting for a nation, which would have the anointing to heal Isaac and Ishmael. I have been waiting for one who will stand to begin to break apart the strategies of the enemy.' And the Lord says to you Canada, 'Will you take it? Will you take your name as a healer of nations and go into the stronghold of the enemy and begin to establish my Jerusalem? Will you do it? Will you heal your nation?'

...I want to tell you one more thing its better to be persecuted for righteousness sake than for stupidity. And so the Lord began to show me something. . . He said, 'I want to release a company of prophets that will prophesy like they would in the Old Testament.' The prophet knew what the king of Syria did in his bedroom. And I want to say to you, listen to me Canada...It's time for the Daniels to raise up for the courts of the king. It's time for the Daniels to be connected to the Prime Ministers. It's time God wants to take us to a whole new level in the Spirit. We want to reach the higher things.

...So the Lord says this is a new day for you. God is going to raise you up in ways that you cannot imagine. The Lord says to you, 'I am going to send you in and you are going to have the heart of a giant killer. I am going to raise up the anointing of David to roll the reproach off the nations (1 Samuel 17:26). Little David said, 'isn't there any one to roll the reproach off of Israel?' The Lord says to you Canada, 'I tried to connect you with the Jewish people when the S.S. Saint Louis came and your forbearers turned them away.' But I would say that, 'there is a day to roll the reproach not only off this nation, you have begun, but you're going to pick up your mantle.' And the Lord says, 'the dominion I will give you to break the powers of division, to break the powers of brothers fighting brothers,

> "I AM GETTING READY TO RAISE A NATION OF RECONCILERS. I AM GETTING READY TO SEND YOU TO THE ENDS OF THE EARTH."

the anointing of reconciliation, the ministry of reconciliation. I am even now getting ready to release you to the ends of the earth.' The Lord says, 'I am getting ready to raise a nation of reconcilers. I am getting ready to send you to the ends of the earth. I will send you to the difficult places.'

The Lord says, 'you Canadian leaders will begin to be known as Norway has been known. But they will come here and they will sign peace agreements,' says the Lord. 'I'm going to use you to bring a lasting peace. But the enemy is at your door and the enemy wants to bring violence in the land, the enemy wants to hurt your land and your children to such a degree that you will get your eyes off the mission that I have placed before you and you will be diverted for another generation.'

So the Lord says, 'Rise up and say...I have decided to stand and fight. I have decided I am going to prophesy! I'm going to evangelize. I'm going to teach. I'm going to come to my place of destiny,' and the Lord says, 'you will go 'from Hebron to Jerusalem.' And I am going to put a reigning anointing upon the head and I am going to put an apostolic anointing on the head.' And the Lord says, 'you will see my anointing go to the ends of the earth,' says the Lord."

Kenneth Copeland, July, 2009
Given At the West Coast Believers' Convention

"This 'Great Awakening' that is hanging heavy over...the nations of the world but most especially in this country and in Canada. This 'Great Awakening' that is hanging there, just hanging there to be realized and to be, to be flowed and released throughout this nation and throughout the nation of Canada, and then in turn throughout the rest of the world.

The prayer, the prayer, the prayer, the prayer that's gone forth. The prayer that is going forth, that's where the power release is. That's where the trigger to these things is, that's the way you release them in your church. And thus saith the Lord thy God, 'In this hour these churches that are teaching and training people to pray of which are on this list and many others also, those are the churches where the explosion and the shekinah glory of God will be manifest first.

The praying churches will walk in it first. And they'll say, 'My, revival broke out over there.' No, answered prayer broke out over there.' The awakening will come out of congregations. There is a hunger in this nation for holiness.

Holiness—real truth, Bible purity before God—and people will run into houses of worship where the glory of God is residing and hanging heavy. And they'll say, 'Clean, clean, clean! Oh to be clean, to be clean.' And they'll run into that atmosphere and My blood will cleanse them from the top of their head to the soles of their feet.

And My Word will take root on the inside of them, and this nation is headed for a Holy Ghost wake-up call. It is on us now—you rejoice, for we'll see it before many hours go by.' Hallelujah."

Rodney Howard-Browne, January 2012

"The devil thought he had the north wrapped up, but God is about to do something in Canada that will shake it from the east to the west and from the arctic to the border - a fire that will spread that will not be put out by the hand of man. O Canada, you shall see the glory of God!"

Lou Engle, February 2012

"I feel the Lord saying it's time to step out of the caves of insecurity Canada.   Come out of the cave with your prophetic calling, and don't see yourself any longer as a little brother. Arise Canada, with the Joseph anointing, for the sake of this nation, America. Take your place. As a nation called for the healing of the nations."

For even more prophetic words that have been spoken over the nation of Canada please visit www.ears2hear.ca.

About The Contributors:

Alain Caron - Alain and his wife Marie are the senior leaders of Le Chemin in Gatineau, Quebec. www.lechemin.ca / www.hodos.ca

Brendan Witton - Brendan and his wife Sharon are the senior leaders of Toronto City Church in Toronto, Ontario. www.torontocitychurch.com

Brent Sloss - Brent and his wife Chani are the senior leaders of Word of Life Regional Church in Guelph, Ontario. Brent is also an author. www.wolrc.org

Bill Prankard - Bill Prankard and his wife Gwen are healing evangelists to Canada and the nations. They are authors and recognized senior leaders in the Body of Christ nationally. www.bpea.com

Derek Schneider - Derek and his wife Mickayla give leadership to History Makers Academy based in Oshawa, Ontario. www.historymakersacademy.com

Doug Schneider - Doug and his wife Judy are the senior leaders of the Embassy Church in Oshawa, Ontario. www.theembassychurch.ca

Faytene Grasseschi - Faytene and her husband Robert give leadership to the MY Canada Association, TheCRY Movement and V-Kol Media Ministries. They are authors, activists and artists who travel internationally as speakers and mobilizers. www.v-kol.com / www.4mycanada.ca / www.faytene.com / www.thecrymovement.com

Femi and Remi Ogunrinde - They are the senior leaders of Lighthouse to All Nations based in Regina, Saskatchewan and travel internationally as speakers. www.lighthousetoallnations.com

Giulio Lorefice Gabeli - Giulio and his wife Lina are the senior leaders of Westwood Community Church in Pt. Coquitlam, British Columbia and Chairs of the Canada Celebrates Israel Network which works with the Knesset Christian Allies Caucus in Jerusalem. www.westwoodcc.ca

Patricia Bootsma - Patricia and her husband John are the Lead Pastors of Catch the Fire Toronto Airport. Patricia leads the Ontario Prophetic Council, is an author and travels internationally as a speaker. www.ctftoronto.com

Patricia King - Patricia is the leader of XP Media, a well known TV personality, author and international speaker. www.xpministries.com

Peg Byars - Peg is on the core leadership team of a key North American Aliyah ministry - Return Ministries, based in Bright, Ontario and Tiberias, Israel, facilitating the return and restoration of the Jews of North America. www.return.co.il

Peggy Kennedy - Peggy is an author. She and her husband Jack lead Two Silver Trumpets Ministries and travel extensively as speakers. www.twosilvertrumpets.ca

Rob & Fran Parker - They are the senior leaders of the National House of Prayer in Ottawa, Ontario. They travel nationally and internationally as speakers and prayer mobilizers. www.nhop.ca

Wanda Fost - Wanda is senior director of Linking Hearts Ministries based in St. John's, Newfoundland - Labrador and National Director of Prayer, Aglow International Canada. She travels nationally and internationally supporting reconciliation and prayer initiatives. www.aglowcanada.com

More Resources Related to Canada or Decreeing Prayer:

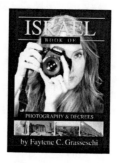

Marked: A Generation of Dread Champions Rising To Shift Nations

Stand On Guard: A Prophetic Call and Research on the Righteous Foundation of Canada

Israel Book of Photography and Decrees

Find the above and other similar resources at www.faytene.com.

Decree a Thing and It Shall Be Established

From the River to the Ends of the Earth

This book can be found at www.xpmedia.com.

This DVD can be attained through Acts News Network.

www.v-kol.com

¹ See prophecies in final section of this book for more.

² Aliyah is the a term to describe the return of the Jewish people to their covenantal home land as described in the Bible.

³ Author Unknown. Retrieved November 2013 from http://www.mts.net/~beamish/P_kennedy_prophecy.htm

⁴ Author Unknown. Retrieved November 2013 from http://www.mts.net/~beamish/P_kennedy_prophecy.htm

⁵ Author Unknown. Retrieved November 2013 from http://www.mts.net/~beamish/P_kennedy_prophecy.htm

⁶ Author Unknown. Retrieved November 2013 from http://www.mts.net/~beamish/P_kennedy_prophecy.htm

⁷ Blom, M & DesMarteau, A. (Producers), 2006, *From the River to the Ends of the Earth,* Acts News Network.

⁸ Blom, M & DesMarteau, A. (Producers), 2006, *From the River to the Ends of the Earth,* Acts News Network.

⁹ Blom, M & DesMarteau, A. (Producers), 2006, *From the River to the Ends of the Earth,* Acts News Network.

¹⁰ Blom, M & DesMarteau, A. (Producers), 2006, *From the River to the Ends of the Earth,* Acts News Network.

¹¹ Blom, M & DesMarteau, A. (Producers), 2006, *From the River to the Ends of the Earth,* Acts News Network.

¹² Blom, M & DesMarteau, A. (Producers), 2006, *From the River to the Ends of the Earth,* Acts News Network.

¹³ Author Unknown. Retrieved November 2013 from http://disciplethenations.org/PropheciesCanada.html#CindyMar04

¹⁴ The fulfillment of this word is already in motion, though more can respond to the call. Shortly after this prophecy was released the MY Canada Association began to launch activists into Parliament and then in 2006 "TheCRY" prayer events were re-launched. Other national ministries such as the National House of Prayer were also launched in this time period. In 2005 there was a shift in federal politics that was triggered by the Quebec sponsorship scandal.

CPSIA information can be obtained at www.ICGtesting.com
Printed in the USA
LVOW05s1920131213

365060LV00007B/27/P